Samuel Fisher Bradford

The Imposter Detected

Samuel Fisher Bradford

The Imposter Detected

ISBN/EAN: 9783743686878

Printed in Europe, USA, Canada, Australia, Japan

Cover: Foto ©ninafisch / pixelio.de

More available books at **www.hansebooks.com**

THE
IMPOSTOR DETECTED,

OR

A REVIEW

OF

SOME OF THE WRITINGS

OF

" PETER PORCUPINE."

BY *TIMOTHY TICKLETOBY.*

" He is a Monster of such horrid men
" As to be hated, needs but to be seen."
POPE.

TO WHICH IS ANNEXED
A REFRESHMENT FOR THE MEMORY OF
William Cobbett,

BY
SAMUEL F. BRADFORD.

Second Edition.

PHILADELPHIA:

FROM THE FREE AND INDEPENDENT
POLITICAL & LITERARY
PRESS OF
THOMAS BRADFORD,
PRINTER, BOOKSELLER & STATIONER,
No. 8, South Front Street.

1796.

TO THE READER.

I HAVE entered into a review of some of the writings of "Peter Porcupine," with considerable reluctance—Neither my engagements nor my inclinations favoured an undertaking, where nothing was to be acquired from a victory over such a despicable opponent. Indeed I felt and could have exclaimed with the poet

"Now by my soul it makes me blush to know,
"My spirit could descend to such a foe."

—Some of my friends, however that I always feel disposed to gratify, prompted me to the task, by an assurance, that contemptible as was Peter Porcupine, he was supported by a *British faction* in the United States, and that it would not be an useless undertaking to pourtray the man who was thus sustained; indeed it has long been my opinion that this pamphleteer was made use of by a *foreign agent* among us, and from his own vindication of himself this opinion has been strengthened into conviction; but his being in foreign pay was not a reason sufficient for me to analize him, had I not been persuaded that he received a countenance from men stiling themselves *Americans*—The extracts which have appeared, in certain Gazettes in the United States, from his writings, carry a presumption, that he is not fostered by a foreign agent alone, that even citizens of America are found prostituted enough to make use of him—The Editor of the Gazette of the United States has even extracted and published from one of his pamphlets, a low and scurrilous attack upon Thomas Paine—a man to whom the United States are much indebted for his exertions during the late Revolution—It was acknowledged then, and cannot be denied now, that the author of Common sense, the Crises, &c. was worth an army to the United States, and yet in the twentieth year of American Independence; a man, who has rendered, such services to his country, is most grossly abused by a *British Corporal*, and this abuse is inserted in a paper which professes itself to be a friend to the American government, to the independence of the United States, and to the cause of Republicanism!!

In the Centinel, a paper published in Boston, Peter Porcupine is actually panegyrised, as will appear from the following extracts from it—
" Mr. *Russel*," The public, of the United States has for some months past been instructed by and entertained with the writings of Mr. William Cobbett of Philadelphia, bearing the signature of PETER PORCUPINE----These writings have been generally read; and the severity of their satire, their lucid argument, and pungent wit, have greatly chaffed the disorganizing faction of our country—Of course the champions of that faction have resorted to their darling weapon scurrility, falshood and Billins-

gate abuse against him---Finding these could have no effect in deterring the PORCUPINE from using his quills, or warding off their barbs, they have been reduced to the pitiful shift of an incendiary and threatening letter—This measure has produced a pamphlet from MR. COBBETT, which a correspondent has enclosed me, in the last mail, and as none of them have yet reached this town, I send you an analysis of part of it, and extracts from the other part, for the amusement of your readers."

" PETER PORCUPINE again.
" MR. RUSSELL,"

My object is to give currency to the writings of MR. COBBETT; *as he has stood forward the Champion of our laws and constituted authorities ;* and notwithstanding his frequent attacks on the *persecuted* PRIESTLEY, and severe remarks on the ruling powers of the French nation---some of which partake too much of the gall of bitterness, those writings have done much service to the cause of federalism, good order and tranquility—I shall now conclude the extracts, which are as follows."

From these extracts it will appear, that Peter Porcupine is considered as the *champion* of our laws and constituted authorities; and altho' he has maliciously and indecently abused " *the persecuted Priestley*," and altho' he has published every vile, scandalous and false thing against our allies, still he is a good federalist and a friend to good order and tranquility! We shall from this be enabled to form some idea of what is meant by *federalism, good order* and *tranquility.* —The man who will use his utmost endeavours to embroil this Country with France—who will propagate the foulest falsehoods and utter the vilest imprecations against her, to accomplish a misunderstanding with her, is a good federalist, is a friend to good order and tranquility." He whose professed object is to extol a nation even to the third Heaven, that has outraged humanity and the laws of nations—a nation that has disregarded our sovereignty, that has robbed us of our property and made slaves of our citizens—such a man is the champion of our laws and our constituted authorities—such a man is a *good federalist* and a *friend to order and tranquility* ! ! Here we have the cloven foot of a British faction, and here we discover the association with a foreign agent to sustain an incendiary scribbler.

The " *lucid argument*" which this Centinel babbler feels such a reverence for, brings to my mind the lines of the poet on a loin of veal in a state of incipient putrefaction, and as it is so analagous, the reader will pardon me for inserting it.

> " So have I seen in larder dark,
> Of veal a *lucid* loin,
> Replete with many a *lucid* spark
> As wise philosophers remark,
> At once both *stink* and *shine*."

TO THE READER.

With respect to the severity of the satire and the pungency of the wit, I will offer no opinion left it might be construed into prejudice; but I will give better authority, the opinion of Peter's own countrymen, the monthly reviewers—In the London Monthly review for 1795, we find the following remarks on the " Observations on the emigration of Dr. J. Priestley, and on the several addresses delivered to him on his arrival in New York."

" Frequently as we have differed in opinion from Dr. Priestley, we should think it an act of injustice to his merit, not to say that the numerous and important services which he has rendered to science, and the unequivocal proofs which he has given of, at least, honest intentions towards the cause of religion and christianity, ought to have protected him from such *gross insults* as are poured on him in this pamphlet. *Of the author's literary talents, we shall say but little*—the phrases " *setting* down to count the cost"—the rights of man the greatest *bore in nature*"—and the appellation of *rigmarole ramble* given to a correct sentence of Dr. Priestley, which the author *attempts* to criticise—*may serve as specimens of his language*."

" *The pitiful attempt at wit* in his *vulgar* rabble of the pitcher harranguing the pans and *jordans*, will gain him *little credit* with *readers of an elegant taste*—No censure however, can be too severe for a writer who suffers the rancour of party spirit to carry him so far beyond the bounds of *justice*, *truth*, and *decency*, as to speak of Dr. Priestley as a man who is an admirer of the massacres of France, and who would have wished to see the town of Birmingham, like that of Lyons, razed, and all its industrious and loyal inhabitants butchered: as a man whose conduct proves that he has either an understanding little superior to that of an idiot, or the heart of a MARAT, in short, as a man who fled into banishment covered with the universal detestation

of his countrymen—*The spirit which could dictate
such* OUTRAGEOUS ABUSE, *must disgrace any in-
dividual and any party."*

The opinions of the monthly reviewers are
corroborated by some " Remarks printed in
London in 1795"—" The same *bad spirit,*" says
the writer, " which persecuted Dr. Priestley at
home, produced *an infamous* and formal attack
upon him from the press, after his retreat to
America; the title of which was " Observations on the Emigration of Dr. Joseph Priestley,
and on the several addresses delivered to him
on his arrival in New York"—In this piece the
writer represents Dr. Priestley as a fire brand,
an open and avowed enemy to the constitution
of his country, &c.—I shall not enter into the
question, whether the pamphlet was first conceived and originated in America or England
—From whatever quarter it issued, it is the work
of a man, who sheweth himself *void of truth and
of every moral principle,* if he were an *English-*

man (and Peter confesses that he is **an English-man**) and if an American, *a gross and ignorant calumniator*" (Thus does the American character suffer by the *trash* imported from the Queen of Isles).

" *But this libellous pamphlet, which was designed to calumniate, did really recommend him, more than a laboured panegyric on his character could have done.* (What honest man that would not think himself honored by the abuse of Peter Porcupine) For the Americans were not wholly ignorant (what civilized country in the world is ignorant) of his writings, and of his being one of the first philosophers of the age, and an eminent defender of the true religion."

There cannot be a doubt that there exists a disposition in certain characters in the United States to assimilate our government to that of Great Britain—Monarchy is the idol of these men, and republicanism of course, their abhorrence and hence the several attempts to establish a monarchy instead of a republic, and hence the propagation of every circumstance with infinite industry, which will add a lustre to monarchy and cast a shade over republicanism—The writings of Peter Porcupine, as far as his capacity extends, go to this point, and hence the patronage which he has received from certain characters in our Country, such for example as his miserable flatterer in the Centinel—To alienate this country from the Republic of France is the first step towards this their favourite object, and hence the dark picture which has been held up of the men and the measures of the Revolution; hence the assertion that the treaty with France is no longer binding. To facilitate their views it is necessary that— some of the worthiest and best men in the U. S. should be rendered obnoxious, that their popularity should be destroyed, hence the scurrility against some of the leading republican characters—All however will not be secure until the late Revolution which gave independence and republicanism to our country can be brought into disgrace, until sunshine patriots, old tories, and proscribed traitors shall have superseded the patriots of 76; hence the traduction of Dr. Franklin, Mr. Paine and others—If the agents of the Revolution can be covered with opprobrium, the Revolution itself will be implicated; for when the props are knocked away the fabric must fall—This is an epitome of the designs of a British faction among us.

It is incumbent on the people to keep a look out. " There is nothing," said Doctor Price, " that requires more to be watched than power; there is nothing that ought to be opposed with more determined resolution than its encroachments." " Sleep in a state," said Montesquieu, " is always followed by slavery,"— We shall not be the first nation that has been undone by supineness, and by the idea that there is no danger—When such men as Peter Porcupine are patronized among us, who will say there is no cause for suspicion? Let the reader examine his works and make his own conclusions—For my own part, I am as solemnly impressed with the belief, that there is a deliberate design to filch the people of this country of their liberties, as I am of the existence of a deity—Would to God I were mistaken! but circumstances, imperious circumstances carry to my mind " conviction strong as proofs of holy writ"—My feelings are tremblingly alive for my Country's happiness, and altho' I had but a small share in the atchievement of our independence, my own and the liberties of my country are dear very dear to me and I feel and could exclaim with the poet,

" ———Is there not some chosen curse,
" Some hidden thunder in the stores of Heav'n,
" Red with uncommon wrath, to blast the men
" Who owe their greatness to their country's ruin?"

The reader will believe me, I trust, when I assure him, that the following remarks were written in great haste—that no attention was paid to stile, and if any inaccuracies occur, this may serve as an apology—My object is not like that of Peter Porcupine, to deceive—I do not write *pour faim*, and therefore I shall be entitled to more credit.

I have never felt the "vinegar mixed with gall" of Peter Porcupine, or perhaps I should have pursued a different mode from some gentlemen with whom he has taken unpardonable liberties. —I mean not to influence Mr. Swanwick, or to substitute my opinion to his; but I solemnly aver, that had such indecent and unjustifiable freedoms been taken with me, I would have answered them as the French gentleman did the abuse of his nation, with a *horse whip*— It would be a degradation of any man of honor to apply this argument himself; but if there was a *negroe* or *scavenger* to be had at the expence of half my fortune, it should have been used—Men accustomed to have their bare backs tickled with a *cat o'nine tails*, would not, perhaps, whine much at the application of a horse whip; but mushroom importance possesses at times a distempered sensibility which makes it alive to circumstances, that would previously have been disregarded—When a villain transgresses the laws, he is punished—Argument to him of his crime, would be like blowing against a North West wind—Society has ordered this matter better, punishment is the argument and it speaks with conviction—It would be equally useless to reason with a man without a sense of decency; being analogous in his feelings with a rogue, no argument so suitable and so much ad hominem as the *argumentum bacculinum*.

THE AUTHOR.

PHILADELPHIA, *August* 26, 1796.

IMPOSTOR DETECTED, &c.

THE Scare Crow commences with a letter said to be written to John Olden, the landlord of this man—This letter bears the genuine likeness of Peter—Let any one compare it with his usual ſtile, his delicacy and his elegance and chaſtity of manner, and it will ſatisfy him that the parent is the ſame—The orthography, it will be ſeen, was ſtudiouſly rendered bad, the more readily to conceal the author; but there is no one of ordinary judgment who will not at a glance diſcover that the writer of the letter was not ignorant of common orthography, whatever might be his moral deficiencies, or his inability in chaſte and correct compoſition—The trick was too palpable to deceive any but the moſt credulous and the weakeſt of the weak—It may be aſked what object the creature could have in view in forging ſuch a letter?—This is pretty obvious—It was nothing leſs than to make himſelf appear of conſequence to his employer and to the faction who countenanced him and to squeeze a little more juice out of the orange—If he could persuade them that he was menaced and in danger, their exertions would be increased in his favour, and thus the stream would receive more supplies—The violence of the letter is another strong evidence of the truth of my assertion—No man is so loud as a coward—no one declaims in favour of honesty more than a rogue and no man so outrageous as the one who wishes to masque his designs. The more virulent, therefore, the letter the greater the chance of concealment, and the greater the presumption of extracting the needful—We have no evidence against this belief but his own assertion, and this of all evidences is the worst, taking it even upon the common credibility of testimony as received in a court of justice—No man is to be admitted an evidence in his own cause, and surely this man would not expect, that his name would stamp a value upon his assertions, when made in his own behalf. —Zanga says, " guilt begun must fly to guilt consummate to be saved," now as there is some similitude of character, and as Peter has fabricated a letter, he must tell a lie to save himself. —This indeed is not very difficult for *him* ; for he can with as much ease say that he is not the author of that letter, as he could assert that he had attended Christ Church for thirty years, or that he owed no taxes—Falshood is his fort, and in this he is rather more dextrous than he was in his *nocturnal peregrinations*.

To obviate the imputation of his being the author of the " cut throat letter" he passes *his* word that *he* was not the writer—Convincing testimony this indeed! The reasons he adduces why he could not be the author are as frivolous as could be adduced, and substantiate his being the author, as conclusively as any circumstantial evidence could do—He talks of the risque he would run of detection at this time? Why at this time? Has he not been "congratulated on his triumph over the once towering but fallen and despicable faction?" Surely then he had nothing to apprehend from a fallen faction! What risque? Has he any reputation to lose? This he certainly must have left sticking to the *post*—Did he dread the vengeance of the citizens of Philadelphia? A people who have shewn so much forbearance in permitting the *refuse* of Old England to mangle the men of the revolution at his pleasure, would not have been excited to violence, by finding such a fellow to be a forger of letters as well as a fugitive from justice and a liar—Had he written it himself " there would have been his hand writing against him" —A wise reason this truly! As if a man who could *forge letters, and do other slight of hand tricks,* could not counterfeit a hand writing for the purpose— " Had he employed another he might have betrayed him"—His old friend Beelzebub surely must have left him in the lurch, or he never would have advanced reasons so superlatively awkward as these—Pray how long was he the writer of Peter Porcupine without being known? He must have found *congenial* souls, or the secret would not have been reserved for *himself* to disclose—Could not the *foreign agent* who employs him, or a number of others of the same political stamp, have furnished an amanuensis for him? Verily Peter thy friend old nick is withdrawing his craft from thee!!! He defies any one to produce an instance of his traduction of the people of the U. S.

—A liar as well as a rogue ought to have a good memory—Peter boasts of the goodness of his; but on certain occasions it is very treacherous—In his "Little Plain English" we find the following delicate opinion of the people of this Country—"When once *the lower orders of the people*, those who have nothing, begin to give law to those who have something, a state of anarchy is at no great distance"—Did this ruffian ever read the Constitution of the U. S.? He certainly did not, or he never would have classed the freemen of the U. S. into orders—Where are *the lower orders of the people* among us? Is it not traducing the people to stigmatize any of them as lower orders? Is it not a libel upon our Constitution to designate any citizens as a lower order? If we have lower orders among us, this *fugitive* is certainly one of them; for he confesses himself that he has nothing, or that he had nothing about the time he wrote that pamphlet—How dare he who has nothing, according to his own confession, meddle in our political controversies? If money is to be the standard of merit or of citizenship, Peter will have very little claim to either, unless indeed his subsidy is more liberal, than his *grade* or talents entitle him to.

He tells us that he has "received letters of thanks and congratulation from every quarter of the Union, even from Richmond in Virginia."—Where is the evidence of this? Peter's word!!! Would any man of common probity take his word after his detection in falshood, and when he knows, that his "*works*," as he ludicrously enough stiles his belchings, are a continued strain of rancourous abuse of the allies of the United States, the Republicans of

France? If he has received letters of thanks at all (which is almost too questionable to make an *if* about), they must have come from British emissaries, or enemies to our revolution; for no friend to the revolution would thank him for vilifying those who were instrumental in its prosperous issue—This assertion carries falshood upon the face of it—How could he receive letters of thanks when he was unknown? It is a well known fact, that till he took a conspicuous stand as a bookseller, the people of this City, much less those at distance, knew not whether he was an highwayman, or a burglar, an ourang-outang, or an Hottentot—He tells us himself that the discovery of the author of Peter Porcupine was reserved for the month of June 1796.—To whom then were the letters of thanks directed? To an anonymous writer? A man unknown—This is too fanciful to be believed now the days of chivalry are past. To those who know the personal feelings of the man it will appear the extremest hyperbole; for till very lately he was agonized at the idea of being discovered—His fears have not yet forsaken him, altho' he had demonstration enough, that "*the dregs of mankind,*" "*the populace*" feel too much contempt for him to make him keep *close house*—He tells us further that he has " received offers of service from persons of the first consequence in divers towns and countries, persons whom he never saw or heard of previous to their communications"—We have not heard lately of any *gangs* in the United States, and we should be indebted to Peter Porcupine to make the communications public, that the persons and property of the citizens might be secured—*Secret* communications of this sort are no doubt made from men of the fame complexion to each other, and thus far credit may be given to his "*precious confeſſions*"—A BAGSHOT may be wanting to encourage timid fpirits, and *a Britiſh Corporal*, therefore, might be fuppofed to poſſeſs qualities to entitle him to "*offers of ſervice*"—What a pity his confcience does not prick him, that he might turn State evidence! —"*Let any fawning ſcribbler on liberty and equality produce ſuch teſtimony if he can*"—It is to their honor indeed that they cannot.

"Again the cut throat fays I have *groſsly* abufed our allies the French—This is falfe—*By the Treaty made between this country and the King of France, the French nation is, in my opinion no more the ally of the U. S. than the Chineſe are.*"—Here is an opinion that founds well in the mouth of *a Britiſh Corporal, and a friend to the federal government and the Preſident of the* U. S. The government has declared that treaty to be binding upon the U. S. but Peter Porcupine fays the French nation is no more the ally of the U. S. than the Chinefe are!—Here we muſt be at a lofs which to be aſtoniſhed at moſt, his extreme impudence, or his extreme profligacy. This fellow has abufed the citizens of the United States for their oppofition to the meafures of the adminiſtration, and yet he has the audacity to come forward and libel this adminiſtration himfelf, by giving a direct lie to their decifion; Where was Peter during the American revolution? Perhaps in the Britiſh army fighting againſt America and her allies—Is it to be wondered at then, that he could declare an inſtrument invalid, made with a nation, who aided us in fupporting our Independence? He would no doubt exterminate that nation as well as the

Treaty, for having embarked in the cause of American Independence. This is the rub—His object appears to be to write down all those men who aided in rendering us independent, not at present in the views of the British Court, and to bring the Revolution itself into disgrace. Hence his abuse of *Franklin* and of *Paine*, and hence his inveteracy against the Republicans of France. It is very obvious, from this declaration, that he would involve us in a war with France, to morrow, if he could, and yet he vaunts of his attachment to our Country and to our Constitution!

Who authorized *a British Corporal* to pronounce upon our national compacts? Is this effrontery grateful to *Americans?* Whatever may be the political mode of thinking of an American, can he relish such presumption? Has the President authorized *him* to judge of our national engagements in his absence, that he is thus free in his decisions? Let this *King-bird* cackle the praises of Louis and his "calumniated Antoinette" till he is out of breath, it would be belittleing an American citizen to interfere in his indulgencies; but let his cacklings be confined to the eulogies of *kings* and *queens*, and not extend to American treaties. I am willing the perfidies of Louis, and the debaucheries of Antoinette should be buried with them, and it illy becomes a *British soldier*, who would have exterminated them both before the Revolution, now to come forward as their champion—Nothing, however, is too abject and too absurd for Peter Porcupine. Of his "*calumniated* Antoinette, the queen of France," Belsham in his reign of George the third gives the following character, "*Diffolute in her manners, unprincipled in her morals, faithlefs in her promifes,* this Princefs wanted only the talents of her predeceffor Catherine of Medicis, to be as illuftrioufly diftinguifhed for *guilt.*" Who will not he extol and who will not he abufe next! I fhould not be furprized to find an eulogium upon BLACKBEARD, the celebrated pirate, iffuing from the prefs of Peter Porcupine.

PETER fays that "*his works are almoft the only works in the United States;*" what a bleffed effect of our penal code! Since the reformation of our penal laws Peter Porcupine's works have become the only works in the United States! It is unneceffary to travel to the dominions of Tufcany for evidence of the good effects of the mildnefs but certainty of punifhment; for Pennfylvania affords an illuftrious example—Here none but the *works* of Peter Porcupine are to be found! It is to be hoped, that ere long, even *his labours* will be transferred along fide of others of a like defcription within the penitentiary enclofure—It appears that even in his beloved Mother Country, his works turned out to as little account as his firft fale of Peter Porcupine, unlefs indeed the *vis a tergo* could be viewed as an advantage—In France his evil genius again purfued him; for even in that land of "*cut-throats*" the works of Peter produced caufe for repentance.

The abufive and contemptuous manner in which this reptile fpeaks of Doctor Franklin ought certainly to excite attention—It is a key which will unlock the whole fecret of his employment—"*Poor Richard and old lightning rod*" —thefe are the epithets applied by a Britifh Emiffary to the parent of American liberty!!

—Even his statue does not escape him; for he says he "deserves to be tumbled from his nich," and this too for the warm testimony which he has left behind him in favour of GEORGE WASHINGTON!! It has already been remarked by a writer, that Peter would vilify the President, as much as he does Doctor Franklin, did not prudential motives restrain him, and this oblique sarcasm on the President is as much a proof of this disposition as he discovered, when he spoke of his official letters, written during the war—On being asked by a gentleman, for the official letters of General Washington he handed him a scurvy edition of them—The person who wished to make the purchase remarked, that the binding of the books was bad—He replied with an air of sovereign contempt, that *it was like the matter it contained!*—Let the people judge from this sample what the fellow would do, if he were not restrained by considerations of another kind than respect. If the people of the United States can tolerate the abuse of *a British Corporal,* lavished upon one of their first and tried patriots, who served them long and faithfully, their revolutionary virtues must be in the wane—If they can countenance such a man, as he asserts they do, we need no further testimony that they are weary of their Independence, and consider their Republicanism as a curse—He scruples not to direct his little might against the revolution and against republicanism, and the man who can countenance such efforts must be a foe to both. The Congress of the United States decreed honors to Franklin by wearing mourning for him after his death—the National Assembly of France, in the time of Peter's beloved Louis, mourned for the loss of this philosopher and patriot, and conveyed their sympathy in a letter of condolence to Congress; the American Philosophical Society paid a tribute to his memory by appointing one of their Members, Doctor Smith, to pronounce an eulogium upon him—even Mr. BINGHAM, who Peter himself stiles " one of the worthiest men in the country," erected a statue to him, and yet this is the character, whom he has selected for his Billingsgate abuse!!—This is " Poor Richard that angels are carrying God knows where"—This is " Old Lightning Rod"!!— This is the " whore master, hypocrite and infidel"—This is the man who " cheated the poor during his life, and mocked them in his death"! His virulence against Doctor Priestley is easily to be accounted for—Doctor Priestley is the friend of a free government, and this is enough to make him an object of Peter's abuse— The Doctor's character is irreproachable, and his literary reputation equal to any philosopher's of the present day. A man who would find fault with him would find spots in the sun, and yet Doctor Priestley has had the honor of receiving the most filthy abuse from Peter Porcupine— and why? because he is not the devoted tool of the British Government; because he dared to think as a Republican ; because he is a man of science and liberality who has embarked in favour of the rights of man ; because he possesses an enlightened and benevolent mind, devoted to the cause of human nature. These are ample reasons for the " vinegar and gall" of a *British Corporal.*

The assertion which Peter made; that he owed " neither the State nor the people of the State a farthing" is an errant falshood; for proof can be made, that *at the time he made the declaration* he owed the county of Philadelphia *two dollars and ten cents taxes*—The collector, Captain Wollpert, demanded payment *since that time*, and not daring now to refuse, he paid his taxes—Let him deny this if he dare—Callous and abandoned as he may be, his effrontery is not equal to it, and why? Becaufe he knows the proof is not on the other fide the Atlantic.

The life and adventures of Peter Porcupine, begin with his hiftory as publifhed in the Aurora, by a writer who ftiled himfelf "*Paul Hedgehog*"—This relation he flatly denies, and endeavours to fupport the denial by an *epitome* of his life, written by *himfelf*, a certificate from Edward Fitzgerald, and a copy of the orders iffued in the garrifon of Portfmouth, on the day of his difcharge. As to his own affertions in his own favour, it has been already fhewn how much credit is due to them—A man, convicted of a lie, as he has been, can expect little charity afterwards, and a forger of letters can eafily turn forger of certificates of recommendation. The account of him given by "Paul Hedgehog," has the appearance of truth about it, and is corroborated by Peter's own account of himfelf: He tells us that his father and grandfather were poor men; fuch was the poverty of his parents, that they could not afford to give him a common education. He ran away from his father and enlifted as a common foldier in the 54th regiment of foot, when, after ferving a number of years, he was difcharged—Some time after his difcharge he embarked for France: Where did he get money to pay his paffage? It will be remembered that by his own account he was advanced no higher than a Corporal in the British army. This *promotion* took place before he embarked for America where he remained till September 1791 " but *a Corporal.*" In September the regiment to which he belonged was sent home; he landed at Portsmouth on the third of November, and on the nineteenth of December he obtained his discharge—*After* his discharge it seems he was made a Sergeant Major, for he tells us nothing about this promotion, till he is about introducing the certificate of Edward Fitzgerald—While he was in " *this new world he was but a corporal*" and from the time of his arrival in England to the day of his discharge, *forty-six days* only elapsed. Is it presumeable that during so short a time he was advanced from a Corporal to a Sergeant Major ? Rapid promotions sometimes take place during a war; but in time of peace the British army is not known for the rapidity of promotion, particularly when there is nothing but poverty as the recommendation. He does not tell us where, and at what time, he was promoted to a Sergeant Major; nay, he does not even breathe that he ever was made a Sergeant, and it is not very common to make Corporals Sergeant Majors over the heads of Sergeants. The story and the certificate, from his own narration, must be supposed a fabrication, a little like the letter sent to John Oldden, and a little like the story of the taxes. As the emoluments of a Corporal in the British Army are not very great, and as he confesses that some of his wages were appropriated towards obtaining books from a circulating library, whence did he derive money to pay his passage to France ? Where did he get money to pay his board during the fix months he remained in France? He does not inform us how he maintained himfelf in France, and it is prefumeable that his earnings in the Britifh Army were not fufficient; how then can we difcredit the relation of Paul Hedgehog? From what fund did he draw his paffage money for coming to America? We cannot fuppofe that he obtained a paffage to this country gratis; from whence then was this money derived? There is fomething very dark about all this Peter, which argues very ftrongly in favour of Paul Hedgehog. A man could not live three months in England, the period of time between his difcharge and departure, go from thence to France, travel many miles in that country, live there fix months, and finally come over to America, upon *nothing*—And yet Peter did all this, and confeffes he was poor, and nothing more than a *Corporal* in the Britifh army. Tales like thefe may pafs down fuch throats as Johnny Bull's, but Americans have not fo large a fwallow—they are not like Shakefpear's blackfmith, open mouthed and ready "to devour a Corporal's news."

Peter tells us a cock and a bull ftory about his father's *penchant* for the American Revolution, from which I fuppofe he means to derive credit to himfelf; but this ftory is *his own*, and has not fufficient marks of authenticity to prove that he was not nurfed in the lap of ariftocracy. "A liar is not to be believed though he fpeaks the truth" is an old adage, and as Peter has eftablifhed a reputation which will bear the application of the adage, he muft not "drench me with vinegar mixed with gall" if I difcredit him—indeed I am entitled to his forgivenefs; for he fays himfelf, that "as to politics, we were like the reft of the country people in England; that is to fay, *we neither knew nor thought any thing about the matter*," and yet he tells us his father was "fo ftaunch an American, that he would not have fuffered his beft friends to drink fuccefs to the king's arms at his table"!!! This to be fure is a good one, but this is nothing for Peter. His father muft have been as much interefted in the American Revolution as Peter is in the caufe of Republicanifm; as his father "neither knew *nor* thought any thing about" the one, he neither knows nor thinks any thing about the other, and thus far he may be faid to be a chip of the old block. It fhall not be my tafk to rake up the afhes of his "honoured and beloved parent," that he ran away from, and treated with the groffeft difobedience and difrefpect. "De mortuis nil nifi bonum" fhall be my maxim, although he, with the malignity of an affaffin, defcends into the confecrated tomb, and feeds upon the dead with the voracity of a tiger.

Peter "hopes, that he may prefume his character will be looked upon as good down to the date of his difcharge. This is prefumption, indeed, after what has paffed. If he had inferted *Corporal*, inftead of *Sergeant Major* in the certificate and the orders, and if he had given an account how he maintained himfelf in England and France after his difcharge, there would have been a better foundation for his prefumption; but, at prefent, it ftands upon very flippery ground. His travels and voyages *without money*, and his promotion to the rank of a Sergeant Major *after* he was difcharged, may make the world prefume that Paul Hedgehog has looked upon him with an accurate eye. He thinks it "*not neceffary to fay how the three months were employed"* in England, after his difcharge, we are, therefore, at full liberty to draw our own conclufions, as he is either afraid or afhamed to give an account of himfelf. He will not fpeak for himfelf, and therefore, Paul Hedgehog muft fpeak for him—

"Peter ftand forth, I dare thee to be tried,
"In that great court where confcience muft prefide."

In fpeaking of PAINE, the author of Common Senfe, the Crifes, the letters to Howe, &c. written during the American Revolution, he fpeaks of a "*Run-away, a Thief, a Tom Paine.*" Why fuch impotent and fcavenger like abufe of Mr. Paine? There is nothing in his hiftory or character which renders him a fit object of fuch miferable fcurrility. Whence then this "vinegar mixed with gall" as Peter terms it; but which I fhould term *Swine's fwill* mixed with *flufh.* Paine diftinguifhed himfelf during the American Revolution. Such was his acknowledged inftrumentality in accomplifhing our Independence, that feveral of the States complimented him with tracts of land. His zeal was great and he was able and indefatigable in his means. To have been an American Patriot is fufficient to draw down the ire of a Britifh Corporal. But this is not all. Paine wrote the Rights of Man, a work of great merit. This work was read with an avidity in England, that made old defpotifm tremble. The miniftry thought the author ought to be filenced, and commenced a profecution againft him. Now the fecret is out. Peter dare not eat the bread of idlenefs. He muft give fatisfaction to his employers, and if he can difcredit Paine, it will

E

answer a better purpose than a prosecution. He may then write, but nobody will read, and the ministry will be revenged. Is not this true, Peter? You may boast of your Republicanism as you do of your honesty; but it won't do, the people can see your long ears peeping out of the lion's skin.

Peter sojourned six months in France, and he acknowledges, that he "met *every where* with civility, and even hospitality in a degree that he had never been accustomed to." Ungrateful wretch! To stigmatize a nation as "*cut throats* and *robbers*" that treated you so kindly! What must the citizens of the United States suppose of this man after such a confession! The principles and feelings which actuate him are no longer concealed; like JUDAS he would betray his master for *thirty pieces of silver*. He denies that he ever spoke disrespectfully of the people of the United States; but who will believe this assertion, or indeed any assertion he could make, after his abandoned traduction of the French People, who *every where* treated him with civility and hospitality in a degree that he had never been accustomed to? As a reward for their civility and hospitality, Peter serves up this same people with the most rancorous abuse, the most contumelious epithets, and exerts the talents and prostitution of a Judas to cover them with opprobrium and guilt! Such a wretch would "thrust his saviour from the wall." What may not the people of America expect when he again returns to his native shore!

Peter insinuates that he "had imbibed principles of Republicanism" and that these principles drove him to America. Shakespeare says "the Devil himself can cite scripture for his purposes," and may not Peter profess Republicanism for his? Let us examine into his republican principles, and we shall find, that like his integrity, they are vox et preterea nihil. In speaking of the people of France, he "ventures to predict, *that sooner or later, they will return to that form of Government under which they were happy, and under which alone they can ever be so again.*" What a republican sentiment! The people of France can be happy only under a despotism! Peter no doubt thinks the people of this Country can be happy only under that form of Government from which they revolted; but as he is in America, and has certain purposes to answer, he has not yet blundered out this opinion. But what kind of a *Republican* must he be, who is of opinion, that a nation can only be happy under a despotism—under a government of Bastiles and lettres de cachets? Peter has annexed some new definition to the term, which we do not understand here; to comprehend his meaning, therefore, we must resort to the context of his works, and then we shall discover, that his principles of Republicanism will suit Algiers, or Morocco, Russia, or Turkey. What a set of accommodating principles for a spy! What a comfortable cullibility for a diplomatic scavenger! His uniform sneers at the "*sovereign people*" as he in derision terms them; the courteous terms of "*dregs, mob, lower orders,* &c. which he in lavish bounty bestows upon the citizens of the United States, speak loudly in favour of his having "imbibed Republican principles"!!!

Peter says he "never was at Paris, as he can prove by the receipts for his board and lodging." This is admirable proof indeed! His own word that he was not there, and if his own word will not do, he can produce receipts ready cut and dry for the purpose. Peter can prove that he was Ambassador to the grand Signior by the same rule; for as he has the nack of manufacturing proofs, he never can be at a loss. He hired a coach to go there, and pray where did he get the money from to pay for it? His pay as a Corporal in the British army certainly did not furnish him with the means to hire coaches. He is very indulgent to his readers; for he leaves them to supply the chasms which dire necessity obliged him to make in the history of his life and *adventures*. This is very kind in him; for they may have an occasional consultation with Peter's acquaintance Paul Hedgehog, who seems fully competent to fill the niches.

And now for the letter from Mr. Jefferson, and what does this prove? That his benevolence would have led him to take a viper into his bosom, which, when warmed by his heat, would have stung him to death. I congratulate Mr. Jefferson on his fortunate escape. His *property* and person have both had an escape. The man who would disgorge such venom against a people, who "treated him with civility and hospitality in a degree that he had never been accustomed to," would have stuck his fangs into Mr. Jefferson the moment opportunity offered; with such a man honor is but a name, and honesty a bubble. An American consul has lately been busily employed in giving passports for France to *British emissaries*, and is it inconceivable that an American agent might have been found in

Holland equally in the British interest, I will not arraign Mr. SHORT's motives. I could wish, however, the man he recommended did not render them suspicious.

Peter has now brought himself to the United States, and here let us attend him, it will be rare sport; for on the threshold he shows his cloven foot. Dr. Priestley is again his mark—"His landing was nothing to me, says Peter, nor to any body else; but the fulsome, consequential addresses, sent him by the pretended patriots, and his canting replies, *at once calculated to flatter the people here*, and to degrade his country and *mine*, was something to me." It has been remarked before that Peter is not the friend of "*the people here,*" and here is proof positive of it—If he " was ambitious to become a citizen of a free state," what were his objections that the free citizens of that state, which he sought as an asylum, should be flattered? He thought " that men enjoyed a greater degree of liberty here than in England," why then did he still consider England as *his country* after his arrival here, and after he had made this country his choice? If the people here were in a preferable state, they were entitled to commendation, and it shows a malignity of disposition to envy it them. If he had forsaken England to take up his residence here, this was his country, and to call another country his, manifests his secret aversion from ours, and proves, that in a collision between the two, he would again mount his shoulder knot in the service of his king. His gall overflows whenever the people of this country are spoken of with respect, and although he sometimes affects to distinguish between them, it is too obvious that he lumps them together in a mass, as fit objects for his spleen. To flatter the people here at the expence of John Bull, was treason in the estimation of this high priest of Moloch, and he would stretch Dr. Priestley upon a bed of torture to revenge himself for it. This is one among other reasons that I have already enumerated for his extreme desire to be the executioner of this great and good philosopher. Had the people of this country still continued under the despotism of his mother country Dr. Priestley would have escaped his malignity for flattering them.

What had a British Corporal to do with addresses to Dr. Priestley? Surely he does not mean to set himself up as *inquisitor general* of the United States, as he has already created himself *interpreter general* of treaties! If he means to thrust the President out of his duties, he ought in mercy to spare the people, and at least allow them the privilege of thinking and acting for themselves in the trifling affair of an address. He talks of the assumption of Democratic Societies; but really, granting all he says of them, they have many steps to ascend before they reach his height of arrogance and insolence.

He seems to feel more against Mr. Carey than he dare express. "My lad" cankers his new born consequence; and if he could get Mr. Carey in a dark and sly corner, I would not answer for the consequences. Was Mr. Carey to blame for his contemptuous treatment of him? Let any man of common discernment survey his "*red head, his lowering brow, his scowling countenance, his brawny figure,*" and by what other term than " my lad" could he accost a wretch who looked like *Jack Ketch?* It was a proof of Mr. Carey's penetration, and he deserves credit for it.

Becaufe he was called "my lad" "*he wifhed for another yellow fever to ftrike the City!!* Gracious God! did nature ever produce fuch another Monfter! I have heard of cannibals, gorgons, furies, devils; but excepting NERO, who fet Rome on fire, and fiddled during the conflagration, I never met with a character before of fuch confummate depravity. *He wifhed for another yellow fever to ftrike the City!!* Citizens of Philadelphia, Citizens of America lend an attentive ear! This is the man, whofe *philanthropy* has brought him forward as a champion of your adminiftration and your Conftitution! What muft be that adminiftration, or that Conftitution which needs fuch an advocate! This man, like Eroftratus who fet the temple of Ephefus on fire to give himfelf a name, is determined to become famous for his infamies. He feems to be the very focus of corruption.

As to his infinuations againft Mr. Bradford, they are merited. When a man will have intercourfe with fuch a being as Peter Porcupine, he deferves all that he chufes to fay of him. That Mr. Bradford *put a coat on his back* cannot admit of a doubt. Peter proves it, and therefore it muft be true; and for this coat put upon his back he has *endeavoured* to put a bliftering plaifter upon Mr. Bradford's. This is his ufual way of requiting his friends. That *a whig* which Mr. Bradford no doubt was, fhould have given countenance to fuch a ruffian, has more than once excited aftonifhment, and now he is rewarded for his apoftacy,[*] as well as for the coat he put

[*] *It is an odd idea, that fome people poffefs, that a Printer cannot publifh a book or pamphlet, but he muft be of that fect, party or faction and adopt all the different notions pre-*

on his back, and the bread which he put in his mouth, before the subsidy commenced. He would have died in a ditch had he not received Mr. Bradford's support, or have become chargeable to the parish.

mulgated therein, be they ever so absurd; and if any of these Wiseacres suppose (as our author pretends to do) that this same printer was once of a contrary opinion, though all the proof they may have of the Change, is, that he has printed a book of a complexion, different to the ideas they would make him entertain, they think they have a right to brand him with the title of Apostate, Hater of Britain, *or any other epithet their ill nature might dictate—Alas! poor printers, how often are ye vilified by these men of Wisdom!*

As our author has granted me the liberty of this page, for a note, I would beg leave to tell him and his antagonist Peter, that though I print both their Lucubrations, I shall not be guided by either and that I approve of neither of their political principles, though could I make them contribute to the good of my Country, or without injury to that, to the emolument of myself, no one would blame me for so doing— That I have made use of the British Corporal—Oh! I ask pardon, Sergeant Major—for a good purpose I have little doubt—Dirty Water will quench fire——

I cannot omit this opportunity, as perhaps it is the only one I may ever think worth embracing, of thanking our British Corporal for his intended blister plaister by his early discovery to the World, that of all the Americans he had ever conversed with, (I fear then Peter thou hast conversed but with few real Americans,) I seem to entertain the greatest degree of rancour against Great Britain. If Mr. Peter will allow me to soften his acrimonious expression, and say, that he has not met with an American, who more keenly feels the wounds his country has received from Britain, or that is more sensible of the injuries she is continually endeavouring to heap on it; I will agree with him. Though I may not be christian enough to love my enemies, yet I may pray for them, that they may see the error of their ways, repent and turn, before it is too late——

Let us now examine Peter's account of the products of his work. The whole amount received from Mr. Bradford was *four hundred and three dollars and twenty one cents*, and upon this he was to subsist himself and maintain his family from the year 1794, to the year 1796, according to his own account. Out of this sum he no doubt paid the *six hundred dollars* which he advanced to his present landlord towards the first year's rent, furnished a book store, and certain other etceteras!!! When the profits of his works were so immense, who would suppose him to be a *British Spy*, in the pay of a royal master? Peter must excuse me for catechising him a little here. I must do it in spite of his vinegar mixed with gall. Pray out of what fund did you draw the money to pay

Were my ideas of Englishmen to be formed from my little acquaintance with this British Corporal, this blessed sample of gratitude, honor, catholicism, good humour and extreme *modesty, I should have little reason to take any of them to my bosom ; but, thank Providence, among the many* Emigrants *he has sent among us, I have reason to believe there are few of worse hearts.*

Lest any of these abusers may still go on with their epithets against the Printer of this essay, I would wish to mention to them, once for all, and whisper it (as you know we must be secret) in the ears of Peter and Timothy, that whatever may be their opinion or sarcasms, that as a Citizen, I have a right, and will enjoy my own opinion, and that as A PRINTER *I shall endeavour to maintain the Liberty of the Press and thro' it the Liberty of my Country, to do which has been the aim and glory of myself and predecessors for upwards of one hundred years ; and that the Liberty of the United States of America may find as strenuous advocates in my posterity, for a thousand years to come, is the prayer of the public's well wisher,*

T. BRADFORD.

your landlord? Who was your banker when you furnished a bookstore? You lived in England three months without any *acknowledged* employment, you passed over to France, hired coaches in that country, lived there six months, came over to America, lived here several years, paid six hundred dollars in advance for house rent, furnished a bookstore, and the only account you give us of your funds for all this, is four hundred and three dollars and twenty one cents! Risum teneatis amici!!! No! no! Peter you never can be in British pay. With such resources as yours, it would be absurd to suppose it.

Peter says he never saw any Agent of the British Government, excepting Mr. Bond, and him he only saw three times in his life, and then he had business with him as an interpreter. Those who choose may interpret this as he did the French Treaty. Were the subject seriously at issue, I could produce as creditable a citizen as any in Philadelphia to prove that a foreign Agent was seen frequently going into his house when he lived in Callowhill Street. What his businfs was with him, I will leave to him to explain. It would be indecorous to say, that he had assisted Peter with the six hundred dollars which he advanced towards his rent, and had furnished him with the philosopher's stone to supply his bookstore, after his positive denial that he is not the journeyman of any of his Majesty's Agents. Perhaps it may be the usual etiquette for his Britannic Majesty's Agents to pay visits to *Corporals*, and the visits which he received may have been only those of ceremony. If this be so, Peter must admit that it smells strongly of *equality* and *sans-culottism*, indeed too much so for a man of *his cut* to submit to.

Peter plays the back sword at Mr. Bond---we understand him, and they, no doubt, understand each other * * * * *

" When a foreign government hires a writer, it takes care that his labours shall be distributed." Very true Peter, and God knows care enough has been taken to distribute your *labours*. My word for it, your labours would not have passed beyond the purview of a printer's devil, or some pardoned traitor, or some hireling of the defender of the faith, or some temple consecrated to secret services, if his Majesty's agent had been unmindful of them.

" Had the Minister of Great Britain employed me to write," continues Peter, " can it be supposed that he would not furnish me with the means of living well, without being the retailer of my own works? Very true—Very true; twelve hundred dollars a year for a house, a large book store that started up like a mushroom in a night, a good coat to your back and now and then a gown by way of change, are paltry things indeed. A man of such fortune, influence and talents ought to have the Minister's privy purse at least at his command. Peter is no subordinate fellow—he would not serve the King, unless he was decorated with all the pomp and splendor which attended one of his Majesty's Ministers in a late mission to China. He possesses too much military pride, and altho' he served as a Corporal in his Magesty's service, it does not follow that he is always to serve him pour l'amour du roi—What! Peter Porcupine in the service of so good and so wise a King, and yet stand " behind a counter to sell a penknife, or a quire of paper" ! ! ! Why his Majesty would think himself disgraced by this; for he makes it a point to pay all his agents alike, from a minister plenipotentiary down to *a spy and a scribbler of pamphlets.* There are no grades in his service—he has no *scavengers,* and like Minister's Plenipotentiary, they are all furnished with the means of living well. Peter's rank in life, his fortune and his importance all prove that he cannot be in British pay, and when to these are added his selling a penknife and a quire of paper behind a counter, the thing must appear impossible. How could he sell penknives and write pamphlets! How could he sell quires of paper and scribble on them himself!

Besides his being an Englishmen would prevent his being useful. This " *would operate mightily against whatever he might advance, seeing the unconquerable prejudices existing in this Country against Englishmen.*" Surely then he cannot be in British pay. In looking over the Scare Crow we find these words " and because I am willing to let slip no opportunity of declaring my respect for a public, from whom those performances have *ever,* from the publication of my *first essay to the present moment,* met with *the most liberal encouragement.*" Again. " I have received letters of thanks and congratulation from *every quarter of the Union, even from Richmond in Virginia,* and not from " British Agents," but from *Native Americans,* real lovers of their Country. I have *received offers of service from persons of the first consequence in their divers towns and countries,* persons whom I never saw or heard of previous to their communications"— And yet Peter avowed himself to be an *Englishman.* In his preface to " A Little Plain English," we have his own word for his being an Englishman. Let him speak for himself—" I dare say, the reader has already concluded that the author of Plain English can be no other than an Englishman; and I *can assure him, the further he advances, the more will he be confirmed in his opinion. It would be useless to deny the fact.* The Democrats have loaded me with every name which they imagine to be opprobrious. (*but of which I am very proud*) such for example, as Aristocrat, Kingsman, Loyalist, Royalist, Clergyman, Englishman &c. it is, therefore, no more than fair play for me to choose from amongst them *that which suits me best—Englishman is the one I have preferred on the present occasion.*" It is not my business to reconcile such incongruities. Peter avowed himself to be an *Englishman;* he declares that he met with the greatest encouragement from the people of this Country, and yet he adduces as an argument that he is not in British pay, because he is known to be an Englishman, and " *the unconquerable prejudices existing in this country would operate weightily against whatever he might advance.*" There is this to be said in extenuation of this most palpable contradiction, that the two pamphlets were written at *different periods,* and that however good his memory may be, it cannot retain every thing!! How true is the old adage that a liar ought to have a good memory. One of two corrolaries flows inevitably from his own statement. Either that he asserted a falshood with respect to the encouragement and patronage he received, or that his works have been foisted into the world thro' some secret agency, and that he is, by means of the same agency, enabled to pay twelve hundred dollars a year for a house, and to furnish a book-store. Peter may take his choice of the two iniquities.

Peter says his " writings have had no other object than that of keeping alive an attachment to the Constitution of the United States, and the inestimable man who is at the head of the government." If the people of this country can read this sentence with the same composure with which I have written it, it will be well for them. A British Corporal keeping alive an attachment to our Constitution is really a good one!!! A man who came to this Country pennyless and unknown, without a single evidence of attachment to our country, a mere adventurer and perhaps a fugitive from justice, keeping alive an attachment to our Constitution, is one of the most unheard of insults ever offered to an enlightened and free people. The Constitution of the United States was the will of the people and of the people only; who told Peter then, that it wanted extraneous aid to keep an attachment to it alive? Did he adventure to this Country for the purpose of interpreting our Constitution as well as our treaties? If any thing could bring our constitution into question it would be such an advocate; for the man who could panegyrise the British Government with all its mighty mass of iniquity and corruption, would blast the reputation of our Constitution the moment his pestiferous breath came into contact with it. Did Peter find an analogy between the two in principle, influence and corruption, that he has turned out the champion of both? The one is a Republic, the other a Monarchy, how could he, then be a friend to both? If he is the friend of a Republic how could he trumpet the praises of a Monarchy?

If he is the friend of a Monarchy, how could he turn the panegyrist of a Republic? The more this said Peter is analized, the more abfurd, the more proffligate does he appear. Principle can have nothing to do with such a man who is every moment at war with himself. The declaration he made when he was charged with injuring the cause he had espoused by his writings, shows the extent of his principles. His reply was " *that he did not care—that he intended to change sides soon, he had come over here to make money out of us, and he did not care how he accomplished it.*" Lest this fine speech might be supposed a fabrication, it has been publicly asserted, that a gentleman of the City, who had been lately a director of the Bank of the United States and a man of unquestionable honor and veracity was an authority for it. This speech carries probability upon the face of it; for the triumphs of the French Republic in Italy and on the Rhine, have converted many a member of the British Faction. Peter has laboured hard in the cause of Mammon without effect. Victory has still been the order of the day, notwithstanding his pamphlets and his prayers; and now he thinks it time to change sides to save his bacon!!! Alas! Poor Peter!

When he was called upon by the tax-gatherer for his taxes during his residence in Callowhill Street, he did not then speak of " the inestimable man who is at the head of the government"— He reviled every man in the government from the President to the Constable, and declared that the people in Great Britain possessed more freedom than we do—This has been asserted in the public prints, and altho' he chose to deny that he owed taxes he did not dare to deny the other part of the ſtory. His ſilence then muſt be taken as a confeſſion of the charge. How ineſtimable the Preſident muſt be in his eyes, appears alſo from the contemptuous manner in which he ſpoke of his official letters. This alſo has been made public, and among his denials this has not been included. What an ineſtimable man is he who is at the head of the Government, in the eſtimation of Peter Porcupine!

It is a hardſhip upon Peter, and he complains of it bitterly, that he ſhould be conſidered as a *foreigner*, not entitled to all the privileges of an American—When he was diſcharging his " vinegar mixed with gall" againſt Mr. Gallatin, he ſeemed to have leſs compaſſion upon foreigners. In this caſe it was a crime to be a foreigner, and his little phial of vengeance was poured upon the devoted head of Mr. Gallatin, for having been born in *Geneva*.

It ſeems from this that he is determined no foreigner but himſelf, or an Engliſhman ſhall be privileged to give an opinion, unleſs indeed he ſhould be a ſycophant or an hireling of Great Britain. A man who avows himſelf a foreigner has certainly no right to meddle in our politics, and as Peter ſtill claims Great Britain as his country, it is the height of impertinence to dare to offer his opinions on the men and meaſures of our Country. Hear him, my readers, and judge for yourſelves. " And if I have give way to my indignation when a hypocritical political divine (ſpeaking of Doctor Prieſtley) attempted to degrade MY COUNTRY, or when its vile calumniators called it " an inſular Baſtile," what have I done more than every good man *in my place* would have done? For a man *in place* under a government, as Peter here confesses he is, to advocate that government may not be confidered as exceptionable; but the impertinence, lies in his interference in our government. It will be remembered, that at the time his gall overflowed in his obfervations againſt Doctor Prieſtley, his beloved countrymen were combined with the favages on our frontiers to aid in cutting our throats; that they were bufily employed in robbing us on the high feas; that they had fucceeded in their endeavours to let loofe the Algerine pirates againſt us; and that they were concerned in many other acts of humanity and good will towards the United States and at this very moment his indignation was excited on hearing *his Country* (not America where he lived and enjoyed protection) fpoken irreverently of!

He afks whether he has done more than his " *duty*" in doing this? It is certainly the *duty* of a man *in his place* to ferve his employers; but was it a part of his duty to meddle in our politics, and throw his ſtink pots at the patriots of the Revolution, and the Republicans in Congrefs? If this conſtituted a part of his duty he has given us the information in feafon. We are now apprized of *his place, his duty* and *his Country.*

This faid Peter Porcupine is made up of blunders. He blunders upon the Editor of the Aurora as the grandfon of Dr. Franklin, to whom Voltaire gave his bleſſing. The fact is that it was TEMPLE FRANKLIN, another of his grandfons. Let us contraſt the account CONDORCET, in his life of Voltaire, gives of the in-

G

terview between Dr. Frankin and Voltaire, with that which Peter has extracted from a *British Magazine*. It will be at least amusing to see the difference of opinion.

" At this same time, Paris boasted, also, the presence of the celebrated Franklin, who, in another hemisphere, had been the apostle of philosophy and toleration. Like Voltaire, he had often employed the weapon of humour which corrects the absurdities of men, and had displayed their perverseness as a folly more fatal, but also worthy of pity. He had joined to the science of metaphysics the genius of practical philosophy; as Voltaire, that of poetry. *Franklin had delivered the vast countries of America from the yoke of Europe;* (this is the rub—eh! Peter) and Voltaire had freed Europe from the yoke of the ancient theocracy of Asia. Franklin was eager to see a man whose reputation had long been spread over both worlds: Voltaire, although he had lost the habit of speaking English, endeavoured to support the conversation in that language; and afterwards resuming the French, he said " Je n'ai pu resister au desir de parler un moment la langue de M. Franklin." " I could not resist the desire of speaking the language of Mr. Franklin for a moment."

" The American philosopher presented his grandson to Voltaire, with a request that he would give him his benediction. " God and liberty !" said Voltaire: " it is the only benediction which can be given to the grandson of Franklin." They went together to a public assemby of the academy of sciences, and the public at the same time beheld with emotion these two men, born in different quarters of the globe, respectable by their years, their glory, the employment of their lives, and both enjoying the influence which they had exercised over the age in which they lived. They embraced each other in the midſt of public acclamations, and it was ſaid to be Solon who embraced Sophocles. But the French Sophocles had trampled on error and advanced the reign of reaſon ; and the Solon of Philadelphia, having placed the conſtitution of his country on the immoveable foundation of the rights of man, had no fear of ſeeing his uncertain laws, even during his own life time, open the way to tyranny and prepare fetters for his country."

This is the Dr. Franklin that Peter Porcupine ſtiles " old lightning rod," and " poor Richard." This is the ſame Franklin to whom he applies every ſcurvy epithet, whoſe philoſophy he ſneers at in the following manner. " *He never made a lightning rod nor bottled up a ſingle quart of ſunſhine in the whole courſe of his life. He was no almanac maker, nor quack, nor chimney doctor, nor ſoap boiler, nor ambaſſador, nor printer's devil.*" Mankind have united in their teſtimony of approbation of Dr. Franklin's philoſophy, and yet Peter, who has neither philoſophy, patriotiſm, veracity, nor principle, has raiſed his pigmy voice againſt millions. Perhaps it would be treating this ſubject as it deſerves, by diſmiſſing it with the words of the Poet, and concluding with him, that

" *A villain's cenſure is extorted praiſe.*"

COPY RIGHT SECURED ACCORDING TO LAW.

A REFRESHMENT

FOR THE MEMORY

OF

WILLIAM COBBETT.

BY

SAMUEL F. BRADFORD.

A REFRESHMENT, &c.

> " The gods take pleasure oft, when haughty mortals
> " On their own pride erect a mighty fabric,
> " By *slightest means*, to lay their towering schemes
> " Low in the dust, to teach them they are *nothing*."
>
> THOMSON.

YOU will, doubtless, be surprised on finding who it is that now addresses you; but, your surprise will be of short duration, when you recollect, that it is one, whose father's transactions with you, all your store of lies and misrepresentation have been expended to present in false coloring. I was at New-York when a gentleman first informed me that the serpent we had saved from perishing had *endeavoured* to sting us. Amazement rivetted me to the spot where I stood—I could not believe it was possible that Cobbett would be guilty of such baseness; that the man, whom I (like an imprudent and unsuspecting youth) took to my bosom as a friend, and treated with every mark of attention and politeness a stranger could expect, would thus reward me; but, however, I found it *was* possible, and do, here, render you my most sincere thanks for the valuable lesson of prudence which you have taught me.

I muſt confeſs that I admired your private character for a long time; but, is it any wonder that a young man, unſkilled in the ways of the world, ſhould be deceived by ſo artful a creature and ſo conſummate an hypocrite as yourſelf. It is beneath the dignity of a man of honor, or of virtue, to be a traitor to his fellow man at all; but, this turpitude receives additional aggravation, when practiſed on an unſuſpecting and unhackneyed youth—However, as you confeſs yourſelf, in your letter to Mr. Bache, that you " *aimed your poiſonous darts at an innocent woman*" (Mrs. Rowſon) it ought not to aſtoniſh me if you ſhould even attempt the murder of infancy itſelf!——

Your public writings, it is well known, I approved ſo far as they reſpected our juſtly celebrated conſtitution, and the Great Man whom the unanimous voice of the people of America has appointed their Chief Magiſtrate; but, as to your principles, *you yourſelf* muſt acknowledge that I deteſted them as much, and even more, than I did thoſe of the party againſt whom your *public* attacks were made. What repeated, what numberleſs arguments have we not had on the ſubject of Republican and Monarchical governments—*Abſolute Deſpotiſm*, and nothing leſs, accorded with your *private* ſentiments: *even the Britiſh Government was not deſpotic enough—it favoured too ſtrongly of Republicaniſm.*

You well know how warmly I defended the cauſe of Republicaniſm; and with what ardor I juſtified the laws and conſtitution under which you *now* live, and which you have ſo frequently abuſed and vilified in my presence: but, all my arguments were in vain—you were " nursed in the lap of Aristocracy." Even the very people, who now treat you with so much attention on account of some of your public writings, have been, in private, grossly abused by you. Our most respectable characters were (according to your account) a set of *Speculators, Land-jobbers,* &c. seeking to entrap and deceive every foreigner who landed on our shores; our industrious mechanics, nothing but a *vile mob, a factious herd,* &c.—The courtly stile of Burke was ever in your mouth.

Call to mind the expression of Mob (meaning the citizens of Philadelphia) which you wished to introduce into the title page of your Plain English, and which my father, with indignation, erased. Deny this, if you dare: even your friend Beelzebub will stare with amazement if you attempt it.

How grossly did you frequently abuse the People of America, by repeatedly asserting that they were, for the greater part, good *Aristocrats,* good *Royalists* in their hearts, and only wore the mask of hypocrisy to answer their own purposes. You even had the vanity to say, you had " *converted many who were staunch Republicans,*" and that you wished your arguments could have the same effect on me; but, that you feared I was too much a Sans-culotte (meaning a friend of liberty I suppose) at heart ever to be reformed by you. This you intended as a disparagement to me; but, I considered it as the highest of compliments; for, remember your own words, " *Men of integrity are generally pretty obstinate in adhering to an opinion once adopted,"*—This maxim, however, my conscience will not permit me to apply to you; for, though "stiff in opinion, always in the wrong," I will not offer such an insult to virtue as to call your obstinacy the offspring of integrity; besides, your reasons were, like some of your writings, mere froth; for, although you can declaim and scandalize with the greatest hero of Billingsgate, yet, in sober argument, and chastity of manner, you are, as far as my judgment goes, the merest nicompoop of the whole group of the defenders of Aristocracy and Royalty—and, in all our numerous conversations, your argumentative powers have proved insufficient to convince me that—" *to be a citizen of America was to be a Slave, and to be a subject to the king of Great Britain, in comparison, a Freeman.*"

There is one circumstance that I give you credit for; that is, the love you bore Old England, and every man must allow the amor patriæ to be commendable. There was no affectation then (as now) of love for America * and a Republican form of government, I mean in private; for hunger (since you have now forced me to tell the secret) made you write in a different style from what you spoke. You knew there was a party here who were charged with an intention to subvert the government, and who were said to be enemies to it; you were then teaching a few frenchmen, in this city, to parler Anglois; (you think proper to make no mention of this in your life; but if

* *No wonder—the stripes on her flag bore too great an analogy to a certain part of your body.*

you have impudence enough to deny it, remember witnesses are at hand) but, finding yourself too dogmatical for a teacher, not of *Boys* over whom you could exercise your tyranny, but of *Men* who would not brook your imperious manner, and fearing to starve, you thought of becoming an author. My father, when you offered him your first productions, saw in them some marks of a ready writer, and *hoping*, (vain hope indeed!) as you were then extremely anxious for concealment, to make you serviceable to his Country and himself, printed them; but, too much of the colouring of your private sentiments would, frequently, appear in your public writings, in spite of the many alterations and amendments we made.

You say in your life that you were " never of an accommodating disposition," in order to prove that we made no alterations in your writings. Your memory is, really very bad " *my Lad,*" or you would not assert falshoods with such unblushing effrontery. Remember what you wished inserted in the New Year's Gift; remember what was erased from the Congress Gallery, and remember, too, the many alterations I made, independently of my father—I would insert some of the erased passages here, but they are too blackguard, too low, and too insulting to Americans, for my pen to write. Yes, Billy, you may thank me for refusing several things which you wished inserted, and especially the piece I made you erase from the manuscript of the New Year's Gift the moment I saw it, and on account of which, if it had been published you would now be, where many a British Corporal has been before you.

Excuse my refreshing your memory with these circumstances; but, I find it is, really, grown so treacherous (notwithstanding your own assertion to the contrary) that I could not avoid it. You have already *" my Lad,"* proved yourself a *Liar* and I can prove you to be a poor pitiful *Coward !*

I well know, that you never expected to receive an answer, or you would not have written what you did. You endeavoured to vilify my father, and, except, in one instance, steered clear of me. You knew my father—You knew he never would stoop to answer the lies of a British Corporal—You knew his character was too well established, and, therefore, you expected your base insinuations would not be refuted. You avoided saying any thing to discredit me; and, every one, who knows your knack at lying, cannot but believe, your fertile brain could have engendered some story or other to injure me, had you not been witheld by *cowardly motives;* yes, I say *cowardly* motives ; for, you were conscious

" I could a tale unfold
" Whose lightest woes would harrow up the souls"— of the freemen of our country.

You, also, knew I was a young man, who had a character to establish in the world—that I was jealous of that character, and, that the least aspersion from you, would produce an answer on my part. This was what you dreaded; and, by saying (as you thought)

nothing to affect me, you expected to save "your bacon"—But you are mistaken. Remember, "*my Lad,*" I am not the heart-breaking rascal to my parents, that you have been to yours. I love my parents—Say you loved yours, if you dare, when you caused them so many hours of anguish. You thought I could read your lies, concerning my father, unmoved, provided I did not come in for a share myself. You did not know me; but, remember, from this time, that every aspersion on his character, I consider as a detraction from my own. Were you to write ten thousand lies, concerning me, I could easier forgive you, than for one concerning him. Let fly your whole store of envenomed Quills against me—I am prepared—Armed with the shield of truth, I fear you not. Methinks I now behold you, swearing vengeance on my head, and biting your under lip 'till the blood almost issues from it. Yes, methinks I see all this; for, though you pretend to have no feeling, I must confess, that when (in our store) you read the *Rub from Snub*, poorly written as it was, you knit your eye brows, shrugged up your shoulders, and " *grinn'd horribly a ghastly smile;*" but, recollecting yourself, you threw it down, and, with an affected laugh of contempt, said " *He's a poor scurrilous dog, and not worth minding.*" Yet, spare me for this time, Billy, and keep your temper a little longer for I have more in store for you—If you do *slaver* a little, only be careful that it does not come in contact with any of your neighbours ! ! !

If any person still doubts your being a *Coward*, he may have further proof in the manner of your attacking Mr. Carey and my father. In order to avoid Mr. Carey's anger, you endeavour to make up with him, by commending his fecrecy. My father, you well knew, gloried fo much in the name of Whig (or Rebel, as you generally ftiled him) that you thought to curry favour with him, and make him forgive and forget your abufe by laying open his principles to the public. He *has* forgiven you; and, has difdained (as you, naturally, fuppofed would be the cafe) to anfwer your infinuations. Nor fhould I (a boy) have honored you fo much had it not been for the opportunity which the preceeding pamphlet offered me of annexing a refrefhment for your excellent memory. I fhall content myfelf, at prefent, with making fome remarks on your *half-told* life and your mifreprefentations and reticence of your tranfactions with my father.

But, to your life—" Set a beggar on horfeback and he will ride to the Devil." Here we fee you, *Mr. Corporal*, mounted on your prickly beaft, cutting and flafhing as you go; friend or foe, it is all one to you, fo that you can belch forth your acrimony and difcharge your rancour.

Whether you were drummed out of your regiment or regularly difcharged (though, by the bye, it is not common to difcharge a good foldier, as you would make us believe) or whether you arrived at New York or Wilmington; whether you remained, in obfcurity, teaching a few Frenchmen to *parler Anglois* in the latter place and afterwards here, or whether you were fkulking in our fuburbs, 'till you fuppofed it was time to flash upon the astonished world, and display your superior abilities, by telling us, that William Cobbett was the writer of certain pieces under the title of Peter Porcupine, I say, these things are matters of little consequence to me. Your insinuations, misrepresentations and reticences are what concern me.

Whether the expression "that my father found you a coat," was really told to you, or whether it was your own consciousness, I will not pretend to say. But this much I will declare, that neither he, or any of the family, ever did make use of the expression; however, on recollection and perusal of your life, the view of your regimentals, which, no doubt, were the best in your wardrobe when you attempted to dispose of your writings, when I view these things, the change in your dress, the addition to your houshold furniture your living down stairs instead of the Garret you were first found in, I make no doubt he contributed to put better cloaths on your back, and better furniture in your house.

Had not my father risked his property in order to print your essays and convince you that his press was free, you might, ere now, have enlisted as a soldier, indulged your love of rambling, or *have been maintained at the public expence.*

You wish to insinuate, page 38, that my father's press is not a free press. This is so false as not to merit an answer. You and your essays prove the contrary, and the people of America well know, that he, as well as his father and great grandfather, have all had the honor of being profecuted for maintaining its liberty in fpite of the frowns and menaces of a Britifh Miniftry. And, while I am its conductor, it fhall be open and free to any and every party, whether in politics or literature; it fhall roll as a free and independent (not licentious) prefs ought to, *in fpite of the clamours of faction, the flander of hirelings, or the frowns of Power.* Nay, were the Prefident of the United States, that firft, that greateft of men, to make an attack on its freedom, it fhould repel him with its native energy.

Apropos, Billy ; I faw at the end of your Scare Crow, " *From the Free Prefs of William Cobbett,*" What ! you have fet up a Free Prefs, have you ?— A Free Prefs of your own too, I fuppofe ! ! Pray, how long is it fince you bought a prefs? You have been very fecret about the bufinefs, indeed: you never let a fingle brother Typo know a word about it, 'till you flafhed upon us with " *From the Free Prefs,* &c." None of the prefs-makers, *here,* had even the leaft knowledge of it, no not one. But, I fuppofe you imported it ; and your workmen too, eh ! for, I have never yet heard of any American journeyman having worked in Billy Cobbett's printing office. At the end of your " Life and Adventures" I do not fee any more mention of the Free Prefs ; the plain imprint " *Printed for and fold by William Cobbett*" is fufficient now! What! fold it already!—Shame on you Billy.—Sell a *Free Prefs* a month after its eftablifhment ! Oh tempora ! Oh mores ! But, to be ferious, as I fee you have repented, if you will promife to continue your good behaviour, I will not tell your friends how you employed another printer, and, plagiarist like, called his press your own; but, mind, this is on condition that I see nothing more of " WILLIAM COBBETT's FREE PRESS."

You say, page 40, your pamphlets were not " honored with the bookseller's name." I see you will be at your old trade of *lying* still. The books, as they now stand in the store will give you the lie. The imprint of " *La Nomenclature Angloise*" says " *Imprimé chez Thomas Bradford*"—but, you forget to place this book in your *very accurate account;* you forget that you ever wrote it, and got paid for it. However, that is no great matter of surprize; it was written for the use of Frenchmen, and you know, that a man, who cannot remember having been a teacher *de la langue Angloise* might, easily, forget receiving payment for a Nomenclature, purposely written to facilitate its acquirement. He might also, with the same ease, forget that he ever wrote a grammar, entitled " Le Tuteur Anglois—— Imprimé chez Thomas Bradford," and that he received a considerable sum of money for it, together with two hundred copies of the work, which he gave his word never to dispose of here (as he had an intention to leave this " *damned country*" and seek his fortune elsewhere) but, which he *did* dispose of to his scholars, and others, at an under price, and thereby injured our sale so much that the chief part of the edition is now on hand, and, if he chuses to purchase, will be sold to him again for half its value.

are both, nearly, of the fame fize. It is true the firft fold better than the fecond; but, he did not know, at the time of making the bargain, this would be the cafe: the prefumption was, that the fecond would have a much quicker fale than the firft, becaufe the writings were more generally circulated and known. Your confcience muft tell you what the 125 Dollars were given for, and, if you have the leaft fpark of honor remaining, you will undeceive a public, already, too much duped by your artifices.

Through your dealings with my father, you cannot fay but that he paid the price you afked for your effays and fome other works which he *hired* you to do; and, perhaps, it might be made to appear you got fomething more; but, the principle bufinefs, your confcience (if you have any) told you, fhould be accounted for was that of the Congrefs Gallery. This, in converfation was ftarted by you or my father it matters not which; but, on conclufion, he afked you what you would have for the work. Your anfwer was, one quarter of a dollar per page. This he agreed to give you, and, accordingly, iffued propofals for fubfcription, as it was intended to be a large work, and continued through the feffion; but, B. Davis, the Bookfeller, who came frequently to our ftore, one day, by popping in, as your were mentioning the Bloody Buoy, difcovered you; and, my father not being over-anxious to publifh it he contracted with you for it. While writing this, you were feveral times applied to for the fecond number of the Congrefs Gallery—you made various excufes to put it off; but, my father, finding you meant to publish the work under another title, called on you, and afked you for the work; you *denied writing*, tho' it was, then, nearly ready for the prefs, and, being preffed, you faid, that if you did write, no other than he fhould have it.

My father had, as far as the word of a man could go purchafed the copy-right of the *Profpect*, and had entered the fame; but you, like an artful villain, finding it had a ready fale, forfeited all ties of contract (fuppofing you an honeft man he had taken no more than your word) and continued the work under another title, as if that would fcreen your villainy. Had the propofals, iffued by him, by and with your concurrence, been filled, the lofs to him muft have been very confiderable; and when the arrangements, made by him, are taken into view, perhaps, had he purfued his ideas (which I am now forry I diffuaded him from) when he wrote the note, dated the 22d of March, 1796, a jury might have given a few pounds damages, to convince a *Britifh Corporal* that he ought to keep his word, with an " *American Rebel*" as well as with any other man!

In page 48, I fee the following fentence " *Mr. Bradford once told me, that Mr. Allen, the father-in-law of Mr. Hammond, faid he was acquainted with me.*" Do you really mean that my father told you fo? If you do, the following exact ftatement will prove either your admirable talent of mifreprefentation, or the *excellence* of your *very excellent* memory. My brother, William Bradford, one day, told you, that Andrew Allen, the son of Mr. Allen, the father-in-law of Mr. Hammond, had, as they were walking together, pointed you out as Peter Porcupine. My father never mentioned the circumstance to you at all; he did not even know it.

I will now proceed to the assertion you make concerning myself. You mention that, Mr. Bradford's son (you forgot I suppose he has three) offered you a hundred dollars a number for the Prospect, in place of eighteen, and that he observed, that their customers would be much disappointed, for, that his *father had promised* a continuation, and *that it should be made very interesting*. The first part of this, for a wonder, is strictly true: I did offer you one hundred dollars, and my father *did promise a continuation* in the proposals; for, as he had your word of honor! for the fulfillment of the contract, he fully expected it would be continued during the session; but with regard to the expression *that it should be made very interesting*, you have fallen into your old failing. I never did make use of it, either to you or any other man, and it is only a fabrication of your own in order to account for your rascally behaviour.

What a pity it is, Cobbett, that you did not entrap me in the Geneva affair. Perhaps you don't recollect this either. I will refresh your memory. Remember that you came across a copy of the history of the late revolution in Geneva, written in French, and that having proposed translating it you wished me to appear as the translator by inserting in the title-page, " *Translated from the French by Samuel F. Bradford.*" Remember too, that you mentioned to me that you designed, also, to write a preface, which was to appear as if coming from me: your intention in fo doing, you hinted, was to make the public (who would compare your ftyle of writing with the preface) take me for the author, and this you fuppofed I would be proud of. Your real intention was to perplex the public opinion and avoid being difcovered; for you were at that time exceffively frightened at the bare idea of fuch a thing. This was the time I began to fee your cloven foot. Do you think you acted as a man of virtue, honor, or principle in endeavouring to draw an inexperienced young man into an affair of fuch a nature? Suppofe, for a moment, I had confented, what fweet nuts you would have had to crack! Thanks to my pride I did not confent. Yes, to my pride, I fay; for it was wounded by fuch an offer. If I had wifhed to become known as a tranflator of the French language or fome other modern ones, I need only to have affixed my name to, and publifhed thofe works and mifcellaneous pieces which have hitherto employed my leifure hours. Perhaps, even now, you do not remember, why you dropt the publication—I will again refrefh your memory: You began the tranflation and intended to publifh it in another name; but, a few days after, you found it was printed by Mr. Fenno, and accordingly gave it up.

I muft now difmifs the fubject, confident I have treated it more fully than it deferved. The time I have been writing the foregoing I confider as loft indeed; but, I could not behold fo many abominable falfhoods with indifference. " *My lad,* " you may now write againft *me* till your " *red head*" turns black.

I here throw you the gauntlet—take it up, and however poorly writen this firſt public anſwer of mine may be, however devoid of all the beauties of ſtyle, and the graces of compoſition the whole of this Refreſhment may appear; yet, you will feel, on reading it, that it contains more *ſtinging* truths than a cat o' nine tails.

You may, perhaps, ſuppoſe, that being a boy, I might forget myſelf and deſcend ſo far, as to honor you with a criticiſm upon your works. No, I diſdain it; your blunders are ſo great that it would be an Herculean labour to enumerate them; your writings are made up of blackguardiſms and grammatical outrages. But, were I to deſcend to criticiſm, I might tell you that the very page which lays before me (49) and which is next to the one from which I but a little while ago made an extract, contains the following elegant and grammatical ſentence. " This we daily ſee verified in the diſtribution of certain blaſphemous *gazettes*, which, though kicked from the door with diſdain, *flies* in at the window." Had I, while at ſchool, written ſuch a ſentence, my ſchool-mates would have hiſſed me from my claſs. *Gazettes flies!!!* Oh! Billy, Billy!!

I will conclude by giving the public your own ſentiments of your own works, which I have in your own hand writing. If you have forgotten this alſo, come and refreſh your memory, or if *you are aſhamed to come nigh our houſe*, get ſome of your friends to look whether or no it is not your own hand-writing. It ſhall be open for the inſpection of the public. Here it is— read and " *grin horribly a ghaſtly ſmile*."

"Mr. Bache,

"A pamphlet has lately made its appearance among us —entitled *A Second part of a Bone to Gnaw, for the Democrats*, which is at once perhaps the moſt impudent and inſolent performance that ever diſgraced a free preſs.—I do not cenſure this piece for its being written againſt the Democrats; for I am certain that every careful peruſer will ſee that its true object is, not to combat thoſe ſocieties, but to vilify all America, and its allies, its faithful allies, and raiſe the intereſts of Great Britain on their ruins. The writer has ſeized the opportunity of a pamphlet containing the proceedings of the United Iriſhmen (which the editor had certainly as great a right to publiſh as he has to publiſh his traſh) to introduce to the unwary public a trait in the French revolution, which, though it muſt give pain to every humane mind, is not leſs excuſable than other exceſſes to which every nation is inevitably impelled by its revolutionary motion. He has introduced this trait, however, with all the exaggerated circumſtances that can be conceived, and while he ſets out with telling his reader that his genius is not adapted to the tragic, he is preparing to " harrow up his ſoul" with horror. But what had the ſeige of Lyons to do with the Democrats in this country or with the United Iriſhmen? There was not the leaſt ſhadow of a neceſſity for introducing it, and it could be done only to vilify the French and *all other republican governments*. Obſerve where the author ſays p 42. " when France was *a monarchy* the common hangman at Lyons entertained a higher ſenſe of honour than has yet been expreſſed by any one of the convention." Is not this inſinuating that it is impoſſible for republicans to poſſeſs any ſenſe of honour? This ſhallow writer has perhaps never heard of the Brutuſes and Catos and of many republicans of modern times that might vie with them.

"The conclusion of this piece bears the stamp of
"its origin; it finishes with endeavouring to persuade
"the citizens of this country, that they ought to pre-
"fer *connecxions* with Great Britain to those with
"France. But this author does not *feel* as an *Ameri-
"can*; the injuries that Great Britain has heaped on
"this country are not imprinted on his heart as they
"are on ours. This reasoning from the present situa-
"tion of France is falacious—whatever may be her mo-
"mentary distresses, she cannot fail in the end to *raise*
"herself superior to all her enemies, and to put to the
"blush all those who are now rejoicing in imaginary
"prospects of her destruction.

"This writer takes particular delight in vilifying those
"characters whom Americans have been long accus-
"tomed to admire—the piece would not be his, if it
"did not contain some sarcasm on the venerable Doc-
"tors *Franklin* and *Priestley*—in this last production he
"seems to have gone a little further than usual, he
"has placed one of them in hell and given us to un-
"derstand that the other will soon follow him.

"His low attempt at wit on this subject can only
"draw a smile of contempt from a man of sense. The
"two great men he has thought proper to treat thus,
"are so far above the reach of his malice, that it
"would be useless for me to attempt their justification.
"The dead have ever been looked upon as exempted
"from reproach, but this pamphleteer disregards de-
"corum; it is not astonishing he who has been base
"enough to aim his poisonous darts at an innocent
"woman, should not look upon the grave as a shelter
"from his malice.

"I shall make but one observation on the stile of this
"pamphlet, it is this; that, if possible, it is some-
"thing worse than any thing this author has before
"given us, and that if this is the way he improves,
"we may expect him to arrive very soon at that per-
"fection of insipidity which will ensure him the title
"of Jerry *Snake*. I would advise him to desist—let
"him leave off while he is well—whatever he may
"imagine, he was never formed to make converts in

[23]

" America—his would-be wit never ceafes to awaken
" difguft, Bone to Gnaw and Grub-ftreet, will foon be
" fynonymous.

A Correspondent

BURLINGTON, June 2, 1795,

"*I have copied this loving epiftle, word for word and letter for letter, preferving the falfe orthography;*" it was written by William Cobbett for publication. He requefted me to tranfcribe it, and fend it to Mr. Bache, which I did; but, whether Mr. Bache's difcernment led him to fufpect the author, who wifhed by *any means,* however *foul,* to bring himfelf into notice, or whether he confidered Peter Porcupine as too contemptible to merit public animadverfion, I will not pretend to fay; certain it is, however, that he did not publifh it. The original remained in my hands, and may now be feen by any perfon who wifhes to behold a fpecimen of *very accurate writing!*

SAMUEL F. BRADFORD.

www.ingramcontent.com/pod-product-compliance
Lightning Source LLC
Chambersburg PA
CBHW020237090426
42735CB00010B/1735